Hardin J Burlingame

History Of Magic And Magicians

Hardin J Burlingame

History Of Magic And Magicians

ISBN/EAN: 9783741152283

Manufactured in Europe, USA, Canada, Australia, Japa

Cover: Foto ©berggeist007 / pixelio.de

Manufactured and distributed by brebook publishing software (www.brebook.com)

Hardin J Burlingame

History Of Magic And Magicians

PREFACE.

The following little pamphlet on Magic and Magicians is not intended to be a complete work on such a vast and interesting subject. It is only to show who the leading conjurers have been in the past ages and their principal feats. Outside of the information obtained during my residence on the continent of Europe in the early '70s and again in '90s, I desire to express my appreciation for information red from Mr. Carl Willman, of Hamburg, Frost's from my friend, Prof. M. Hermann, of Berlin. future time the work may be taken up

· H. J. B.

HISTORY
...of...
MAGIC AND MAGICIANS.

Who is there who does not remember the first magical performance he ever witnessed? We recollect distinctly that the doors had no sooner opened than we were the first to buy tickets and taking our seats a full hour before the performance was to commence, waited impatiently and with a beating heart till the curtain should rise in front of this world of wonders. And when the marvelous performance commenced, when eggs changed into dollars, dollars into pocket handkerchiefs, bird cages disappeared in the air, and empty boxes held numerous presents, then we lived in a land of dreams far away from earth.

Nowadays it is quite easy to look behind the scenes of a conjurer. A number of dealers in, and makers of conjuring apparatus will sell you everything in this line the heart can wish for ; wands, cups, rings, balls, prepared cards, and many other things too numerous to mention, and all "ready for instant use, accompanied by full and complete instructions." Books without number, from the cheap ten cent "sell" of a circus pamphlet to the fully illustrated manual elegantly bound, offer to initiate you into the mysteries of the black art. But all these books and directions, with only a few exceptions, tell you only of what the trick consists, and not how it's done, without regard to the fact that just the most interesting tricks are kept secret by the adepts or sold for a high price.

In order for us to arrive at a clear understanding of Magicians and their works, we must begin at the beginning, or in other words, go back, almost to the primeval man. Space will not allow us to take up the early history of magic, or its supernatural features or tendencies with which it teemed in the dark ages ; the scope of the present article is the practical part of magic and its exponents, as applied to the furnishing of harmless and pleasing entertainments. Let us consider first the Indian jugglers and necromancers.

How thoroughly they were skilled in magic is shown in an ancient Persian manuscript written by Emperor Jepang. In it, he describes the operations of Indian jugglers who had been asked to show their tricks for the amusement of the court. The emperor was so astonished at the wonders created by these men, that he was forced to ascribe to them supernatural powers.

First they were asked to raise on the spot ten mulberry trees from a corresponding number of seeds. They placed the mulberry seeds in the ground in different places and in a few moments a mulberry tree began to spring from the earth, and every tree had leaves, branches and fruit. Trees of all kinds were produced in the same manner, and they all bore their fruit, which the emperor declared to be very good. Before the trees were removed there appeared among their branches birds of marvelous beauty in their color, form, and in their songs. Finally it was noticed that the leaves of the trees took on the last tints of autumn, and gradually, as they had appeared, the trees sunk away from the spot where the conjurer had created them.

Incredible as this story seems, the ornithologist, Major Price, assures us that he himself witnessed similar performances on the west coast of India. But he noticed that a cover was used to conceal the operation, and hence thinks that the jugglers carry with them trees in all stages of development, from the tender plant of a few days to the fully bearing. Major Price has undoubtely hit upon the right solution of the mystery.

Unfortunately most travelers who publish reports of such occurrences lack the necessary knowledge of magic to judge and interpret rightly what they have seen.

If numerous scholars who travel the world over as investigators would find out such conjurers' tricks, they would see at once that it is wise to suppose they make use of simple means and not such as belong to the supernatural. Not long ago a scholar described an experiment which he had himself seen performed by an Indian juggler.

Twelve or fourteen persons, of whom nine belonged to the troupe, formed a circle, in the centre of which stood a basket. A juggler having lain himself in the basket, was covered up. The form of the juggler dwindled more and more and finally when the cover was removed the basket was found empty. The basket was again covered and the juggler reappeared in his former place. The traveler states that he could not explain this occurrence, the more unable to do so as there was no depression in the ground beneath the basket, the juggler was unprepared as the trick was performed in front of his host's residence. He further adds that he had often seen experiments by European magicians, but had never been so mystified.

This is the opinion of a man about a thing of which he knows nothing, and hence he cannot understand it.

When he says that the trick approaches the supernatural he arouses in the reader a disposition to look upon it in the light of superstition and instead of explaining, produces an opposite effect. If he had been perfectly conversant with the tricks of these conjurers, and had had a thorough knowledge of magic, he would have known that there is always means by which a person may be spirited away without the use of a hole in the ground, or a secret passage. For a conjurer who travels with professional companions it is an easy thing to perform the above mentioned trick, if you consider that he only works to perform an illusion. And it is for this purpose he travels with companions.

How easily the public may be deceived is proven by a similar experiment of the clown, Tom Belling, called August, and performed for many years in Renz's European Circus, and always to the greatest astonishment of his audience. He would place a table in the middle of the arena, ask a lady to step upon it, and then cover her with a wicker frame of paper. Twelve footmen, one after the other, passed through the frame. Then the performer took the frame from the table and the lady had disappeared. The explanation is very simple.

One of the footmen was disguised as a lady; inside the frame he would quickly discard the lady's habit and walk out as a footman. It was not noticed that one more footman came out than went in, because as soon as one came out, he joined the others standing in the arena.

The lady's dress was carried out in pieces by the several footmen, who found means of concealing them about their person.

If Tom Belling had spirited the lady away from the table without first covering her, then it would have been a surprise.   He needed accomplices, without which also the Indian conjurer would have been helpless.

The second assertion of the above named traveler, viz., that this performance was superior to that of modern magicians, has also no foundation.

The modern European or American magician is much better educated than his colleagues in other lands, and therefore he is able to perform much more deceit.

To be able to judge this you must know magic thoroughly.

The progress in science at its highest in Europe, has enabled the magician to practice his art to a greater extent than among less civilized nations.   But it is a known fact that a person sees more wonders in a foreign land than in his own.

The suppleness, perseverance and physical strength of Inbian jugglers is well known.   Fane states that in Delhi he saw several men jump into a well thirty metres deep, for a rupee thrown to them as an inducement to attempt the hardy feat.   In Madras the people of this class are noted for the suppleness and flexibility of their bodies.   For an example, they experience no difficulty in winding themselves in and out through the rounds of a ladder.   In the same manner, having reached the top he again winds his way to the bottom. The ladder all this time being perfectly balanced in an uprightposition, without support of any kind.

Tennant in his work on Ceylon, gives a lively description of some juggler's tricks, which he had the opportunuity of seeing on the road between Colombo and Candia.   The juggler stood upon a pole six feet high, and in this insecure position, the pole being unsupported, except through his poising, caught pebbles which a person threw him from the ground.

When he opened his hand, instead of the pebbles being seen, birds would fly out and away.   He broke an egg shell out of which crept a snake, and he juggled with a large number of metal balls, using his hands and elbows.

These are performances which require a certain knowledge of illusion, as well as dexterity and remarkable flexibility of joint.   They occupy but a small part of the science of magic, which employs the hidden powers of nature and technical secrets.

Going back to the original subject of magic we are confronted with the query, what is its origin? And we must admit that the cradle of magic was carved from the wood ot. India.

Magic found its most favored soil among the Medes and Persians. Their " wonder-men " had the name of " Megh " from which is derived the Greek word " Magus," and hence the word " magic " itself.

Soon magic spread over Greece and Italy and in the middle ages over Arabia. Taking advantage of man's cupidity for gold, and his craze for this precious metal, magic adopted the special field of gold-making and alchemy, thus taking the place of the earlier use of astrology in order to satisfy human curiosity in prying into the future.

Even in Munich in 1590, the two dogs of the magician Bragandino were found guilty of witchcraft, and condemned to death. The last official adept was the pharmacist, Boetticher, who however made porcelain instead of gold. His death occurred near the end of the last century.

With the Portuguese, St. Germain and the Count Balsamo Cagliostro, magic enters the modern age of jugglery. Although both were magicians and conjurers, they also appeared as so-called prestidigitateurs. Enlightenment fought constantly against the more notorious productions of this fictitious world. The practice of magic as a business had to be abandoned, and its practice threw off more and more of its garb of deceit.

The magicians of the first half of our century, such as Pinnetti, Compte, Grise, Dobler, Bosco, Anderson, Phillipe, Robert Houdin and others, all took the modern point of view, and labored rather to make magic appear as apparent only, and used a particular branch to entertain.

The old time juggling was happily metamorphosed, magic taking its place. Still there remained unpleasant remnants of the old superstition, under the name of spiritualism, because the world is not satisfied with the ideal manifestation of spirits, but must have something tangible, and the useful humbug is always there to fill the pockets of its adherents.

The fifteenth and sixteenth centuries were flourishing times for quacks, mountebanks and charlatans, to whom belonged Paracelsus, Agrippa von Nettesheim, Faust, and later, Mesmer, Dr. Eisenheart, Cagliostro, Dr. Graham, and others. The most celebrated of these mountebanks of the middle ages was undoubtedly John Faust, born at Knittlingen, in Wurtemburg, or according to others, in Saltwedel, in Altmark.

At the time of the Reformation several adventurers traveled around under this name, which accounts for the different opinions as to his birth place. Faust learned magic in Cracow, in Poland, and undoubtedly he was initiated into the so-called spiritualistic tricks. In Erfurt, before professors and students, he materialized the spirits of Homer, Hector, Achilles, Polyphemus, and Helena. It is related of him that at the inn of Knittingen, he ate up a boy, drank a whole tub of water, and later on produced the boy from behind the stove.

In Madgeburg he performed his tricks in the market place. Claiming that he did not get enough money of the audience and did not care to stay any longer in the company of such ungrateful people, he said he was going to Heaven, and suddenly throwing down the reins of his horse, the latter began to ascend heavenward. Faust took hold of the horse's tail, his wife took hold of his coat, the servant clutched the skirt of his wife, and thus together they ascended to Heaven, if we are to believe his historians.

He was followed by the noted adventurer, Notre Dame, better known by the Latin name of Nostredamus. He was born in the city of Remy, in Provence, about the year 1503. He was of Jewish extraction, and from two of his ancestors, inherited the profession he later followed. Both his grandfathers were celebrated physicians and astronomers, one was a physician to the king of Jerusalem and Sicily, and the other had a similar position with the Duke of Calabria. The former educated his son for a doctor and initiated him into the mysteries of astrology.

Later the young man studied medicine at Montpelier, fled from the pest epidemic and settled at various places throughout the country, performing wonderful cures. Of the different kinds of necromancy, he practiced principally that of sooth-saying at the birth of a child, reading according to the position of the stars its future destiny. After having obtained fame in this branch, he practised all the arts within the limits of prophecy; he made the weather for the farmers, determined the time for planting and for harvesting, told fortunes, and designated the spot where stolen goods might be found.

Nostredamus had good luck and gained great honors.

He conceived the extravagant idea of prophesying to the world in print the density of nations and states, and like the Greek oracles he gave his predictions in short sentences, and preferred to clothe them in poetic figure rather than in direct expression, and thus from his rhymes one could read that which suited him best.

The publications of his prophesies took place in 1555, at the desire of the queen, Catherine de Medeci. The prophet was called to Paris, invited to court, and loaded with presents. In a short time the second series of prophesies were printed. This time he dedicated his work to the king, who presented him with his portrait engraved on a gold medallion. Finally he was made court physician and astrologer, although in this office he did not predict any important events, not even the premature death of Henry the Second.

Philadelphus Philadelphia was the name of a celebrated conjurer who flourished in the latter part of the last century and who traveled very extensively through Germany, exhibiting his tricks in all the leading cities. His real name was Jacob Meyer. His tricks were very striking, particularly to the ordinary spectator who believed that the effects were accomplished by the performer being able to cause a temporary blindness of his audiences.

This belief was very agreeable to Philadelphia, who did all he could to strengthen the belief that he was a real magician or conjurer of witches. During his travels he stopped at Gœttingen, noted even at that time for its universities.

During his stay there a peculiar advertisement appeared on the streets. It was a large wood cut and consisted of a large globe representing the earth, on the top of which was standing a ladder reaching up into the heavens. The Hoiy

Trinity was represented standing on this ladder. On the top round was the Father with a bow in his hand and in the act of shooting an arrow to his left. A few rounds below, the son was seated, and below him a dove.

Frightful appearing angels looked down through the surrounding clouds. On each side and a little lower the resurrection was shown, the figures and forms having claws. The redeemed ones on the right side resembled frogs, and were illuminated by a light from the heavens. On the left side were the doomed chased by the imps of Satan and pictured as being seared by lightning from the clouds, and threatened by the arrow from the bow of the Father.

This most peculiar thing, devoid of all taste, was used as a ridiculous preface to an announcement of Philadelphia. At the foot of the sheet was an ancient cut of the city of Gœttingen, the particular feature of which was the church towers with their weather vanes. This printed sheet contained the following announcement :

By request ; (third edition) Advertisement :

"All admirers of supernatural physic are hereby notified that the world renowned magician, Philadelphus Philadelphia, who was mentioned by Cardamous in his book, ' de-natura supernaturali,' as the one envied by heaven and hell, has arrived here by regular mail, although it would have been just as easy for him to have come through the air.   It fact, he is the same person who in the year 1482, on the public market in Venice, threw a ball of yarn up into the clouds, and then climbing the cord of yarn disappeared into the heavens.   On the 9th of January this year, he will begin to show openly and secretly his one dollar tricks in the town halls, and will weekly advance to his better ones until he at last reaches his $500.00 tricks, among which are found some, that without talking nonsense, far exceed the most wonderful, in short, as might be said, worse things are impossible.   He has had the honor to appear before all the high and low potentates of the earth, and appeared last week, and also four weeks ago, before Queen Ohera in Otaheiti, before whom he produced his tricks with great honors and applause.   He can be seen every day, excepting Mondays and Thursdays.   He cannot be seen between eleven and twelve in the forenoon, as he is at that time engaged in Constantinople, and he is not visible between twelve and one, as he dines at that hour.

Of his many wonderful every day dollar tricks we will mention but a few, not particularly the best ones, but those which it takes the fewer words to describe.

1st. Without leaving the room he will take the weather vane from the top of St. Jacob's church, and place it on the spire of St. John's church, and vice versa the vane from St. John's and place it on St. Jacob's. When they have remained in this position a few moments they will each return to their original positions.

N. B. This is done by simple dexterity and without the use of a magnet.

2nd. He will take six ounces of the purest arsenic, grind it to a fine powder, boil it in two quarts of milk, and treat the ladies present with it. As soon as they begin to feel the evil effects of it, he will give them a few teaspoonfuls of melted lead to drink and all will go home laughing and in the best of humor.

3rd. He will take a stick of wood and strike a bat on the front of its head until it falls down dead. While lying on the floor he will strike it another blow, when it will stand up and coolly ask, "what music is that I hear," and become as healthy and perfectly well as before.

4th. He will pull the teeth of several ladies, and one of the spectators may then mix them up together in a sack, then load them into a shot-gun and fire off the charge at the head of the ladies whose teeth were pulled, and they will immediately find without pain or knowledge of the charm that their teeth are back into their proper places, solid and as ivory white as before.

5th. A metaphysical effect, whereby he shows that something can be, and at the same time cannot be. It has caused a prodigious expense of time and money and he shows it solely for the benefit of the university, for one dollar.

6th. He will take all the watches, rings ane jewels from those present, also the cash, and when it is desired will give a receipt, then, *with all these things thrown into a trunk take his departure.* In eight days each person will tear their receipt in two, and as soon as this is done the watches, rings and jewels will return again.   He has earned much money with this trick.''

Philadelphia read this dodger, which had undoubtedly been put out by a rival conjurer, and as a result disappeared on his journey between night and morning.

Philadelphia came from a Jewish family in Philadelphia and when he joined the Christian church he adopted the name of his native city.   At an early age he showed an inclination for mathematics and physics which brought him to the notice of Duke Henry of Cumberland.   After the latter's death he gave mathematical-physical performances in England, and in most all of the countries of the Continent.

A Hamburg professor, has in his possession an original program of Jacob Meyer's which was used at the appearance of Philadelphia in Luneburg, and from this it can be seen that his wonderful tricks consisted only of simple experiments, which would scarcely be shown now-a-days.

Among them were card tricks, the so-called Egyptian clock, Bacchus with the wine barrel and the magic ink stand.   Philadelphia would place Bacchus on the table and pour a glass of pure water into the barrel.   Then he would ask the spectator if he wished wine or brandy out of the cask and the figure of Bacchus would tap from the barrel the desired drink without any help from the artist.

The ink stand consisted of a thin cup in a pretty wooden case, which turned on the top.   The inner part had from ten to twelve compartments partitioned off by tin walls in the shape of a star.   Every compartment was filled with a different colored ink and the pen was dipped through a hole in the lid of the stand.   By turning the lid the hole through which the pen passed could be brought over any of the compartments, and the pen dipped into any kind of ink.

These hints serve to show how simple the whole trick was.

Nevertheless Philadelphia obtained great success on his numerous tours, and even with people of high standing he made much of a reputation.   He made a great deal of money and enjoyed his trips practicing magic.   He traveled throughout Europe, performed before the Empress Catharine, and won the favor of the Sultan Mustapha Third at

Constantinople. Later on he had great success in Vienna and Berlin, and also in Potsdam before Frederick the Great, after which he retired to private life.

The stars were less favorable to a comtemporary of Philadelphia's, the famous magician, Count Alexander Cagliostro.

He came from a merchant family in Palermo, and manufactured the cognomen of "Count" from an aunt, as he needed a title to carry him through the world, his real name being Jos. Balsamo.

While in a convent in Palermo, he learned of an apothecary something of chemistry and medicine but abused the knowledge.

In different tours through the East he perfected his dexterity and became proficient in all kinds of tricks, also learned the art of forging documents and seals and practiced with zeal the profession of the idea of "mine and thine."

Later on he met in Rome the beautiful daughter of a saddler and as she was dexterous in the practice of sly arts and promised to be a good assistant to him and helpmate, they were married. She was indeed more inventive than himself, especially when there was a chance to play the comedy of life.

He had a practice of changing his name to suit his tricks, never told his birthplace, his extraction, or his age, but would tell the people that he had been a guest at the Wedding of Cana.

That he had lived before the deluge, and that he had been in the ark with Noah.

On the whole Cagliostro played the part of a magician, prophet, and exorcist so well and with so much skill, that people of the better class, scholars and writers met him with great deference.

The ladies wore fans, hats and souvenirs a la Cagliostro; his wife's picture and his own were worn in lockets. Marble busts of the couple were to be seen in the parks and palaces, and under the picture of the charlatan were inscribed the words, "The Divine Cagliostro."

One of his arts was the preparation of a rejuvenating tincture by whose use the old and wrinkled ladies might obtain a smooth skin and the various charms of youth. He also prepared an universal essence for the cure of all diseases. If his customer was rich enough to pay a large sum he would even cause the dead to reappear and disembodied spirits converse with mortals and divulge the secrets of the grave. As the founder of a certain mysterious lodge Cagliostro gained many adherents. He led his brotherhood back to Henoch and Elias and promised the members that they should be born again, morally and physically, and in that way they could live 5,000 years.

In Paris, Cagliostro enjoyed the friendship of Cardinal de Rohan—in Petersburg his "noble" wife shone as the Princess Santa Croce—in Warsaw he was received by the nobility as a prince, and in the province of Kurland they formed a plan to offer him a principality.

In France where Cagliostro had his first success his star began to wane. He was accused of having had a part to play in the well known affair of the diamond necklace, the great fraud of Countess Sawotha, a lady in the Court of Marie Antoinette.

Cagliostro was taken to the Bastille in 1785, and after a short term of imprisonment he was banished from the country. He fled to London, and later to Italy.

But instead of his former successes he had bad luck everywhere. In May, 1789, he gave his last seance. His swindle was discovered and a few months later, Dec. 2nd, 1789, he, with his wife, was thrown into a dungeon of the Inquisition.

He denied all the crimes imputed to him, but his wife made a full confession, out of fear for torture. He was sentenced to death, but this sentence was commuted to life imprisonment by Pope Pius.

There are different versions of the manner of Cagliostro's death, but it has been proven that he died Aug. 28th, 1795, from apoplexy, in a prison cell in Rome, or more correctly, in the Fort St. Leo.

We now enter upon the consideration of the magicians of the present century, at the beginning of which magic appears in the form of harmless entertainment, and its representatives are honest performers of their art, surprising and amusing the public through delusion, and naturally expecting adequate compensation for their trouble and skill displayed.

One of the earliest representatives of this class was Bartholomew Bosco, born in Turin, made the trip of the campaign in Russia with the French armies, was taken prisoner and went to Siberia, where he attracted attention by his astonishing tricks in magic. He was discharged in 1814, and taking leave of a military life, traveled for eighteen years through Europe and the East, practicing his art most successfully. He was the first magician who made his experiments with simple apparatus, and declared them to be natural experiments. His apparatus was very simple indeed. They consisted of tin cups and paste board boxes, some of which are still extant.

Bosco died March 6, 1863, in Gruna near Dresden.

His son followed in the footsteps of his father, but had the misfortune while performing in Weimar, to shatter his hand by the explosion of a pistol.

The magicians traveling now under the name of Bosco have adopted the name purely for advertising purposes.

For the same reason many magicians are not satisfied with their own name but try to pass for foreigners, as they find a great majority prefer a foreign name.

We should not forget to mention Prof. Louis Goldkette, a prominent Danish conjurer and founder of a well known theatrical family. He was born in 1778, and died in 1833. For years he traveled over the continent and performed with much success before nearly all the Royal families.

The great magician Hermann had like Bosco a long and lasting fame, and his name has been adopted by many imitators. He himself, Compars Hermann, generally known as Carl Hermann, died at 70 years of age, July 8th, 1887, in Carlsbad.

He was without doubt the most noted of modern conjurers. Without using much mechanical or optical apparatus, he produced many wonderful effects by a sharp observation of the absence of mind of the human auditor, assisted by a hand as firm as steel and capable of the most deft movement. Hermann was the son of a traveling conjurer and was probably born in Poland, January 23, 1816. At an early age he went to Paris where he perfected himself in the French tongue. In 1848 he began his professional tours and traveled throughout the world reaping both fame and fortune.

He knew Patagonia as well as his city of Vienna, and was as much at home in any city of Spain as in his own neighborhood.

From his first marriage in 1854, to the singer Csillag and from whom he was separated four years later, he had a girl, who is at present known in America, as the opera singer, Blanche Corelli.

Hermann found his domestic happiness with his second wife, a Frenchwoman, Mlle. Ernest, whom he met in Gibraltar.

Hermann reigned supreme for years in Austria and Germany in the domain of higher magic, and there was scarcely a European court where he was not a welcome guest. He took pride in showing his friends the invitations of potentates, written with their own hands, bidding him welcome in the most flattering terms.

Everywhere he received costly presents. From the city of New York he received many souvenirs, among them an acknowledgement of his charity performance, a gold medal as large as the top of a silk hat. He was a passionate collector, but did not keep his collections together. He was restless, would sell his collections and again begin the collection of new curios. He lost a fortune several times—once in the panic of 1873; but came again to the top, and died a millionaire. He was noted for his charities, and for his free, honest, and frank life He was well informed, and liked to talk on different subjects. His sharp eye had also a very good natured expression.

In his presence one was unconsciously reminded of the saying of a French gentleman and journalist on the appearance of Hermann, " Mephisto bon enfant."

The following is a programme of one of the last entertainments given by this celebrated performer.

CASINO AT WIESBADEN.

Tour of the celebrated Prestidigitateur, Prof. C. Hermann, under the management of Mr. A. Morini.

—†—†—†—†—†—

Monday evening, July 19, at 8 o'clock.

Extraordinary Performance of the celebrated Prestidigitateur, Prof. C. Hermann, of Vienna.

1st Part.	2nd Part.
1. Everybody's Card.	1. The Obedient Cards.
2. The Canary Islands.	2. The Flying Watch.
3. The Chinese Egg.	3. The Omelette.
4. The Miser.	4. Quicker than Lightning.
5. A Mistake.	5. The Ring in Danger.
6. " The New Creation.	6. Catching Fish and no Fish.

—:—:—:—:—:—

All of above experiments are inventions of Prof. Hermann, and are executed without any apparatus or parapharnelia.

Tickets, 75c and $1.25.

—:—:—:—:—:—

There are very few among the conjurers of the nineteenth century who have anything like the fame of Hermann.

Among these few we name Prof. Liebholz, who was not a prominent sleight of hand performer, but who nevertheless excelled in performances of extraordinary nicety and accuracy.

He started a new direction in modern magic; the general use of apparatus or mechanical instruments of all kinds.

He worked out many new ideas, and had the apparatus made by different mechanics. Innumerable tricks of Modern Magic,—the Indian basket, Hindoo Box Trick, the Speaking Head, the Sphynx and many others, were first introduced by him.

In the use of his ideas he had a great influence on the science of mechanics and its profession.

In Hamburg he ordered of Oscar Lischke, a wood turner, many pieces of apparatus, boxes, nine pins, plates, cases, etc., and soon the turner had a good trade in these articles.

· In proportion as his success increased, the wider grew the circle of amateurs, and the number of Liebholz's colleagues, who were quick to find out the profitable business he was doing.

Lischke who supplied these amateurs was not a mechanic himself, but employed other workmen, and they in their

own behalf endeavored to further interest the people in
magic.

In this way Hamburg through the influence of Liebholz,
became the birthplace of modern magic and no city in the
world has as many amateurs as this city on the Elbe.

Next to Hamburg, Nurnberg is the most important
manufacturing city of magical appliances. In the beginning of 1870 magic took another direction. All double
bottoms, double cones, pasteboard boxes, etc., were laid
aside by the better class of conjurers, and they only performed the finer drawing room tricks with invisible appliances.

From this time on magic became fitted for use in the
drawing room and on many of the programmes we may read
that they perform their tricks without covered tables and
without visible apparatus. At the time Liebholz was giving
his attractive performances, there existed the magic theatres
of the three Dutch brothers, William, Ernest and F. T.
Basch, who surpassed their great predecessors so far as stage
setting went. All were performers of the old school who
made a great showing on the stage with ornate apparatus.
They travelled chiefly through Holland and made a great
fortune.

William Basch, the eldest and most celebrated, is now
dead.

Prof. Hartwig Seeman traveled about the same time with
a magic theater. Seeman came from Stralsund, and later
gained quite a name and experience in India, he being the
first of modern conjurers to visit that far away country.

He returned to Germany with apparatus all of solid silver, and was considered the richest magician of his time.
He appeared in his act literally covered with diamonds, and
the suit that he wore on the stage was valued at 50,000
marks.

Later he traveled in Sweden and Norway, came in the
beginning of 1880 to the United States and died in Texas in
1884.

Other representatives of the old school in Germany of
late years have been Prof. Mellini, St. Roman, Agoston,
Becker, Lorgie and Bellachini.

Mellini is a brother-in-law of Prof. Basch, and had a

similar theatre. Of late years he has performed at the various fairs in the cities of Nurnberg, Frankfort, Cologne, Madgeburg, Leipsic and Vienna.

He usuallly had a tent elegantly ornamented in the interior and met everywhere with great success. In 1886 he visited a fair in Leipsic for the last time as a conjurer. He then gave up the business of magic and undertook the management of a theater at Hanover.

Agoston traveled with a similar theatre through Germany under the title "Chevalier Agoston." In the 60's he had a ship turned into a magic drawing room, and traveled in this floating palace, up and down the Rhine, stopping at all the cities along this river and giving performances. Later he visited all the larger cities of Germany and Switzerland. He is noted for the interest of his ghost shows, which he produces with elegant settings. Mrs. Agoston afterwards appeared as a magician in Oriental costume, and had surprising success.

Prof. St. Roman, whose real name is said to be Stroman, also belongs to the category of these artists. He performs in theatres built especially for that purpose, as well as in halls, and is considered a very dexterous performer.

He has performed at many courts and possesses many marks of honor in the form of gifts. He resides in Vienna, owning several houses there, and travels through all countries with some novelty. His greatest effect is the "duck hunt," and this has never been imitated with the same elegance and accuracy with which he produces it.

Prof. Becker, born in Berlin, also belongs to the list of above named artists. He has traveled for many years with an elegantly arranged theatre and has met everywhere with great success.

Knowing the Russian language, he has travelled principally in that country, and in Poland, in which countries he has had less competition. He is for Russia what Hermann was for Germany and Austria, the most prominent and famous artist of modern times.

Prof. Lorgie is a resident of Hamburg, where he owns a magical theatre, and he seldom goes outside of the limits of his native town. He has made a few trips to Russia, but as a rule visits only the cities of East Prussia, Mechlenberg,

Hanover, Holstein and Denmark. Every year he returns
to his native place at the time of the Dom, a fair which lasts
about four weeks at Christmas time, and occupies with his
theatre the same place his father had in the market place.

Bellachini, whose real name was Bellach, was born in
Poland, and was an officer in the Prussian service. In 1846
he took up magic and succeeded in making for himself both
name and fortune.   '

He performed mostly in Germany, beyond the limits of
which country he seldom passed, winning there the title of
"Court Artist."

He himself tells that at a performance before the Prussian court he used the magic ink stand to the astonishment
of all the court and Emperor William I.   He handed his
majesty a pen and asked that he convince himself that he
could write in any desired color, and the Emperor asked,
"but what shall I write?"   The performer quickly
requested him to write "Bellachini, Court Artist," and the
Emperor laughingly did so.   The next day he received
his diploma as "Court Artist."

Many jokes are told of him, quite a number of which
are true.   Very often on the first night of his performances
he would appear in a travelling suit, as if he had just
arrived, and would take off his overcoat and gloves and
begin with the words: "Unprepared as I am."   Sometimes when showing a trick with a handkerchief he would
turn to the audience with the words: "Does any one
happen to have a clean handkerchief?"   And of course all
would laugh.   Bellachini seldom performed tricks requiring
dexterity, for he could scarcely make a dollar disappear.
But he was supplied with all modern apparatus, which he
worked by electricity and mechanism, and he also did a side
business in magical apparatus, which he sold to amateurs as
a "particular favor, at cost prices only."

Among modern German performers Prof. Bellachini was
acknowledged to be the most perfect and elegant of all.   It
is true that he did not invent anything whatever in magic,
but whatever he executed or performed was perfectly done.
He was a thorough representative of magic and conjuring.

Yet, notwithstanding his successes, he left but very little
when he died, in 1880, of a stroke of apoplexy, which
attacked him during one of his performances.

A later generation of magicians such as Prof. Stengel, Neubours, Max Rossner, Charles Arbre, Robert Alexander, Schradieck, Jacobs, Miss Eleonora Orlowa, and others, belong to the class of latest hand and drawing-room artists. Charles Arbre, whose real name is Carl Baum, is the foremost among them. He was born in Olmutz (Maehren). He is one of the few conjurers who have received an extra fine education, being not only a clever gentleman, but a conjurer par excellence. He is also the inventor of many wonderful pieces of apparatus, which have found the greatest applause wherever shown.

The Court Artist, Max Rossner, who greatly resembles Arbre has made great progress and stands to-day among the most important of his profession. He was born in Dresden, and after serving his military school-time, began his artistic career.

A few years ago he married and enlarged his business and he promises in time to be the most celebrated of Germany's talent in this line; he is now preparing for an extended tour of Russia.

Prof. Stengel, who was formerly a traveling Tyrolese singer, has also achieved some celebrity in magic. Honored by many of the court princes, he has also received the title of Court Artist. His home is in Wiesbaden, and in the summer time he makes trips to the watering places along the Rhine.

Prof. Roberts is a finely educated artist, and is distinguished for his intelligence and marked dexterity. He also has a talent for making beautiful combinations and his delivery is very fine.

The most celebrated card performer of the world is undoubtedly Dr. Hofzinser, of Vienna. He was a government employe, and as he could not appear publicly as a conjurer, he established a theatre in Vienna under the name of Madam Hofzinser. He was an educated gentleman, having received his diploma as a doctor, and his manipulation of cards has never been excelled.

A very worthy pupil of his is George Heubeck, also of Vienna. He is the only one who took up the mantle of Dr. Hofzinser and was worthy enough to follow in his footsteps, and is, without exception, at present, the greatest living sleight-of-hand performer, but is now so old that he has retired entirely from the practice of the art.   In spite of the phenomenal dexterity, which was born in him, he did not understand how to create for himself a better fate and is now living in very poor circumstances.

We should not forget to name Ben Ali Bey, the inventor of Black Art.   His original name is Autzinger, and he was born in Bavaria.   For seven years he was an actor in one of the Berlin theatres and as he could hardly support his family on his small salary, he looked around for something else and seized upon the original idea of Oriental Magic.   His invention was first shown in Berlin, in Castan's Panopticum where it received very little notice.   Shortly afterwards the attention of Arbre was called to it, who visited the performances several times.   He saw a chance of improving it and engaged Ben Ali Bey to go with him.   The first part of their performances was parlor magic.   In the second part Ben Ali Bey introduced Black Art and in this representation he made his reputation.   The success was so great that it was imitated immediately by the entire profession all over the world, but none of them succeeded in producing it any length of time, as they were all very poor imitators of the original.   Ben Ali Bey is to-day still traveling with his Oriental Black Art, and wherever he makes his appearance he is crowned with the greatest of success, and much to his honor it must be said that no person has yet been able to introduce Black Art as well as he has done.

A striking figure among modern German conjurers is that of Bruno Schenk.   Born in Breslau in 1857, he entered upon a commercial career, occupying his spare time in studying conjuring, and succeeded so well that in 1876 he gave a charity performance in Breslau that was attended by over 3,000 persons.   This was enough; the young man hung up his office coat and became a professional conjurer.   As such he travelled with varied success through Germany, Austria, Hungary, Russia, Sweden; sometimes "flush" and often "broke," till at last he succeeded in establishing his renowned Eden Theatre, the only one of its kind in existance.

He has played before Kings, Queens and Princes almost without number, his Eden Theatre (which we would call a travelling theatre) from its stage to the utmost corner of its gallery, is a work of art. The costliness of the carpets, decorations, stage fittings, the elegance of this entire portable building is something unequalled, the only one of its kind in the world. While Bruno Schenk has had greater predecessors, no one has ever equalled him in such a magnificent fashionable theatre or produced illusions in better manner or with more elegant surroundings. He is now in the full tide of success.

The best representative of modern years in Paris has been Prof. Carmelli, a young gentleman who performed there during the last exposition. He appeared dressed in a red swallow-tail coat, and in his manner was exceedingly peculiar, as he combined parlor magic with the Black Art on the same darkened stage. He combined parlor magic tricks with the wonders of the Black Art in such a manner that his representations were really unexcelled. It must be admitted that the French performers seem to be really born for the art of prestidigitation. They stand alone in the elegance of their manner, and the attractiveness of their language, in executing their tricks.

A conjurer well-known through France is Prof. Antonio, who executes everything he does without a mistake and in a brilliant manner. He is a very small gentleman, but overcomes this apparent obstacle with much neatness and skill in his manipulations.

Of the female magicians in Germany, not a few, Eleonora Orlowa has so far met with the greatest success. She was the adopted daughter of Prof. Becker, whom she assisted on the stage, but later made a start herself, and with great success. In the beginning of the 80's she retired from the stage to married life.

In a branch of magic, in the performance of certain experiments, especially in this country for a spiritualistic purpose, many female artists have worked with a great deal of skill.

In latter years Miss Anna Eva Fay is the most prominent. She allowed herself to be tied hands and feet, and then placed in a close position and while in this restraint will play on musical instruments, nail boards, cut out paper figures, and write with a pencil.

Quite a celebrated conjurer among the fair sex is Madame Cora, an American lady, from Ohio, and the first one to tour the far east from here. For about twenty years she has been travelling in all countries practicing this particular branch of the theatrical profession. The following is her programme as produced at Singapore, on the island of Java.

TOWN HALL, SINGAPORE.

PROGRAMME

of

MADAME CORA'S

PARLOR ENTERTAINMENT

for

Thursday evening, 2nd August, 1888.

PART I.

Overture　　-　　　-　　　-　　　-　　　By Miss Cave.

MAGICAL ILLUSIONS by MADAME CORA.

1. The Travelling Merchant.
2. The Law of Resistance overcome.
3. The Magicians mode of interchanging property.
4. The Separation and Transposition of Wine and Water.
5. The Mesmerism of the Dove.
6. Illustration of Animal Magnetism.
7. Making matter animate by the same power.
8. The Occult Cabinet.
9. The Marabout Mocha.
10. The Protean Sheet.
11. Mysterious Treasury of the air.
12. The Ladies' Favourite.
13. The Enchanted Frame.
14. Rope tying a la Davenport.

INTERVAL OF TEN MINUTES.

PART II.

Overture - - - - By Miss Cave.

The Couch of the Angels, in which Mdlle. Louise will be placed in a Mesmeric state by Madame Cora, and made to represent Beautiful, Historical, and National Tableaux, as follows:

Red Riding Hood, Angel Gabriel, Amazon, Britannia, Erin, Scotia, America, Mercury.

—:—:—:—:—:—

GOD SAVE THE QUEEN.

Let us now retrace our steps and see what was being done in England during the time the conjuring profession was being developed on the Continent.

The first professor that claims our attention is a French conjurer by the name of Comus, who commenced his "physical, mechanical and mathematical recreations" in a large room in Panton Street, London, England, at Christmas, 1765. Before this time there were probably humble professors of the art, frequenting the fairs, or "pitching" in market places or on village greens, but their names and performances have not been recorded. Comus announced that his stay in London would be limited to fifteen days, but he prolonged it to three months, giving two performances daily, at twelve and six, and charging five shillings for admission. It may be inferred, therefore, that he found his visit profitable.

The social position of the professional conjurer was at this period even more dubious than that of the actor. The prejudice against his art and its professors which had been born of ignorance and superstition was dying out with the process of mental enlightenment; but he was ranked, in common with the juggler, the posturer, and the tumbler, as a vagrant, and in his provincial ramblings was sometimes in danger of being treated in that character with the stocks. He might be patronized by the upper classes, and even by the royal family; but he was not admitted into good society, or even regarded as a respectable character. They were often confounded with fortune-tellers, and suffered in repute by the error,

The next one to appear in professional circles was Mr. Breslaw, who gave his entertainments in Cockspur Street, with great success for nine successive seasons; but after 1773 it was sometimes given on alternate evenings at other places; in 1774, in the large ball-room of the King's Arms, near the Royal Exchange; in 1776, at Marylebone Gardens; and in 1779, at the King's Head, near the Mansion House.

In 1776, Breslaw reduced the admission fee to half a crown for all parts of the room in Cockspur Street, and to two shillings at Marylebone Gardens. His conjuring entertainment was at this time interlarded between the first and second parts of a vocal and instrumental concert; and this plan was adhered to in the three following seasons. In 1777 he introduced his "new sympathetical bell, magical clock, and experiments on pyramidical glasses." He was always absent from the metropolis during a portion of each year, when he made a tour of the provincial towns.

After exhibiting his tricks in London for eight years successively, he seems to have found it necessary to apply a stronger stimulus than before to the popular organ of wonder, and in 1779 his announcements gave a fuller view of his performances.

"Between the different parts," says one of his advertisements of this year, "Mr. Breslaw will discover the following deceptions in such a manner, that every person in the company shall be capable of doing them immediately for their amusement. First, to tell any lady or gentleman the card that they fix on, without asking any questions. Second, to make a remarkable piece of money fly out of any gentleman's hand into a lady's pocket handkerchief, at two yards distance. Third, to change four or five cards in any lady's or gentleman's hand several times into different cards. Fourth, to make a fresh egg fly out of any person's pocket into a box on the table, and immediately to fly back again into the pocket."

Flockton, better known as a successful showman than as a conjurer, used to perform some conjuring tricks on the outside of his show, to attract an audience; and, with Lane, Robinson and other small fry of the profession, attended the fairs in and around London for a quarter of a century. In 1769 he gave a variety entertainment for some time at Hick-

ford's Concert Room, Panton Street; but conjuring does not
appear to have been included in his programme. The fees
for admission ranged from six pence to two shillings. The
same prices were charged in 1780, when he prefaced an exhibition of FANTOCCINI with a conjuring entertainment
at a room in the same street, probably the same that was
afterwards occupied by Breslaw.

Flockton is said to have been a poor conjurer, but he
contrived, by means of his wonderful clock, his FAN-
TOCCINI, and his performing monkey, to accumulate five
thousand pounds, the whole of which he divided at his
death between the various members of his company, who
had traveled from fair to fair with him for many years. He
died at Peckham, where he always resided in winter, in
1794. He bequeathed his show, and the properties pertain-
ing to it, to Gyngell, who had latterly performed the conjuring business, and a widow named Flint; but within a
year after his death the whole interest in the show was
possessed by the former.

Of Robinson, the conjurer, there is no record but the
name, which is mentioned in a newspaper report of the visit
of the Duke and Duchess of Gloucester to Bartholomew fair
in 1778. One of Lane's bills is preserved in Bagford's collection of NOTABILIA relating to that fair, now in the
library of the British Museum; and his feats are therein
shown to have been varied by posturing and dancing by his
two daughters. All that can be gathered concerning Lane's
tricks, however, is contained in the following morsel of
doggerel rhyme:

"It will make you laugh, it will drive away gloom,
To see how the egg will dance around the room;
And from another egg a bird there will fly,
Which makes the company all for to cry,
'O rare Lane; cockalorum for Lane; well done, Lane;
You are the man."

Another of the conjuring fraternity was Katterfelto,
whom Cowper described as—

"With his hair on end at his own wonders,
Wondering for his bread."

Katterfelto, whatever his pretentions to skill and dexterity as a conjurer may have been, was the first of the pro-

fession, since the time of Faust and Agrippa, to give a philosophical character to his entertainments, and avail of the resources afforded by science for the purpose of illusion. He commenced with a philosophical lecture, which occupied an hour, and was followed by an entertainment of two hours duration, a different lecture and series of experiments being given on each evening of the week.

The next name with which the records of conjuring presents us is that of Pinetti, an Italian who came to London in 1784, with the reputation of having performed before several crowned heads on the continent, and received certificates of merit in their royal hand-writing. He engaged the Haymarket theatre for the winter season, and announced, in a larger advertisement than the conjurers of that day were wont to issue, that he would, "with his consort, exhibit most wonderful, stupendous, and absolutely inimitable, mechanical, physical and philosophical pieces, which his recent deep scrutiny in those sciences, and assiduous exertions, have enabled him to invent and construct; among which Signor Pinetti will have the special honor and satisfaction of exhibiting various experiments of new discovery, no less curious than seemingly incredible, particularly that of Madame Pinetti being seated in one of the front boxes, with a handkerchief over her eyes, and guessing at everything imagined and proposed to her by any person in the company."

This is the first instance that we have been able to discover of what has since received the name of clairvoyance, or second sight, being introduced in a conjuring entertainment, for which purpose it was so much used by Anderson and Robert Houdin more than half a century afterwards.

The death of Pinetti furnished a London journalist with a theme for witticism which, though ill timed, was conceived in the professional humor of the conjurer. "Poor Pinetti, laid in his coffin, finds death is no conjurer;" wrote the humourist; "and that he never suffers to escape, by sleight of hand, the bird which he once confines in the box."

Another famous conjurer of this period was Rollin, grandfather of the late political celebrity of that name, who was minister of the interior in the provisional government of France of 1848. After accumulating a fortune by the ex-

ercise of his profession, and purchasing the chateau of Fon-
,tenay-aux-Roses, in the department of the Seine, Rollin in-
curred the suspicions of the committee of public safety in
1793, and suffered death by the guillotine. On the war-
rant for his execution being read to him, he turned to those
about him, and observed, "this is the first paper I cannot
conjure away." He left two sons, each of whom, after the
fall of Robespierre, planted a cedar in the courtyard of the
paternal mansion, where the trees have since grown to
magnificent dimensions.

A second Comus—for he can scarcely have been identical
with the French conjurer of that name who was contempo-
rary with Jonas—appeared early in June, 1793, at No. 28,
Haymarket, London, as then announced, "for one week
only," but prolonged his stay for "a few nights more," until the middle of July, charging half a crown for admission.
He had previously made the tour of the provincial towns
with considerable success. His programme was divided into
three parts, the first of which consisted of an exhibition of
magical watches and sympathetic clocks, and the others of
the tricks which now constituted the ordinary REPERTOIRE
of the conjurer, but after the first week, he condensed the
latter into the opening part, exhibited in the second, "the
invisible agent for the interchange of thought," which had
been a leading feature of the entertainment of the original
Comus, and comprised in the third "various uncommon
experiments with his Enchanted Horologium, Pyxidees
Literarum, and many curious operations in Rhabdology,
Steganography and Phylacteria, with many wonderful performances of the grand Dodocahedron, also Chartomantic
Deceptions and Kharamatic Operations. To conclude with
the performance of the Tereto-pæst Figure and Magical
House; the like never seen in this Kingdom before, and
will astonish every beholder."

Comus was a skillful coiner of the hard words so affected
by conjurers, and some of the productions of his mint would
puzzle a Cambridge professor of Greek. It may be well
therefore, to inform the reader that his Thaumaturgic
Horologium was, as described by him, a self-acting machine
—the only one then existent—which, "by the means of an
Alhadida moving on a Cathetus, discovers to the company

the exact time of the day or night by any proposed watch, although the watch may be in any gentleman's pocket, or five miles distant, if required; it also points out the color of any lady or gentleman's clothes, by the wearer only touching it with a finger, and is further possessed of such occult qualities as to discover the thoughts of one person to another, even at an unlimited distance."

Another of the number of the minor entertainers of that day, was Moon, of whom Raymond tells an amusing anecdote. The conjurer arrived in Salisbury one night, at a very late hour, during Elliston's engagement at the theatre of that city, and took up his quarters at the same inn. Stratford, the manager, had accompanied Elliston to the inn on leaving the theatre, and, after a bottle of wine had been drunk, proposed to call up the landlord to take a hand with them at loo. Moon at that moment entered the room and was immediately invited to sit down with them.

"I should be most happy to do so, gentlemen," said the conjurer, whom neither of the gentlemen had ever seen before, "but unfortunately, the state of my purse—"

"Never mind;" cried actor and manager together, "we'll lend you a few guineas."

Moon's hesitation disappeared immediately, and he sat down, expressing the sense which he felt of the kindness and fellowship of gentlemen to whom he was a stranger. Five guineas were advanced to him to begin with, and play was commenced with exhuberant spirits. Elliston and Stratford soon found themselves losers; Moon paid them the five guineas he had borrowed, and still the run of luck was against them. When they arose from the table neither of them had a guinea left.

"You will give us our revenge?" said Elliston.

"With pleasure," returned the conjurer.

"I shall be in Salisbury again, this day week," observed Elliston.

"I am sorry," said Moon, "to be obliged to disappoint you, but I am engaged that night at Devizes, to cut a cock's head off."

"Cut a cock's head off," repeated the actor, regarding the conjurer from head to foot; "have we been playing, then, with a decapitator of the sultan of the dung hill? Who are you, sir?"

Moon handed a card to Elliston, who read aloud, with his characteristic solemnity of countenance and voice, " Mr. Moon, celebrated conjurer, whose dexterity in command of the cards is unanimously acknowledged, will undertake to convey the contents of any gentleman's purse into his (Mr. Moon's) pockets with surprising facility. He will also cut a cock's head off without injuring that noble bird."

As Elliston raised his eyes to the countenance of the conjurer, upon which a slight smile played, the latter bowed, and withdrew from the room, leaving the actor and Stratford regarding each other with looks that cannot be described and only a Cruikshank could portray.

An equally clever conjurer of this period, was Torrini, whose real name was DeGrisy, under which he originally appeared. He was the only son of a French loyalist noble, the Count de Grisy.

Young DeGrisy, being thrown on his own resources, studied medicine, and endeavored to establish himself in that profession in Florence. Failing there he moved to Naples, where he became intimately acquainted with the famous Pinetti, and learned to perform all his tricks and deceptions. He gave several amateur performances, and won great applause from the friends who witnessed them; he was finally persuaded to give a public entertainment for the benefit of charity which was to be attended by the royal family and many of the Neapolitan nobility.

This performance, though it was a lamentable failure, was, he always asserted, the cause of his adopting conjuring as a profession.

For sixteen years he conjured with success in various parts of Europe, but at the end of that time his fame began to wane, and he discerned the necessity of introducing some startling novelty. Unfortunately, he determined to present the gun trick in a new form, himself representing William Tell, and shooting from the head of his son an apple, from which he afterwards took a bullet, supposed by the spectators to be the ball fired from the rifle. He was performing this trick at Strasburg, when, by some fearful mistake, the leaden bullet was fired from the gun, and the unfortunate youth fell dead upon the stage.

This horrible event produced temporary insanity in the

unhappy conjurer, who recovered his reason only to undergo his trial for homicide, which resulted in his conviction and six months imprisonment. His wife died during his incarceration, and the poor conjurer, on his release from prison, would have been friendless and destitute but for the exertions of Torrini. Taking that name to conceal his identity with the convicted homicide, he set out for Bale with as much of his apparatus as had not been sold or pawned during his imprisonment; and after a short tour in Switzerland, returned to France and died at Lyons from a fever.

In 1814 some clever Indian jugglers performed in London, at a room in Pall Mall, and repeated their performances during the three following years in the principle towns of the United Kingdom. One of their feats was the gun trick, in which one of the performers pretended to catch between his teeth a leaden bullet fired from a pistol. By a terrible fatality, the poor fellow lost his life while exhibiting this trick at a place of amusement in Dublin. The pistol was, according to custom, handed to a young gentleman, one of the company, for the purpose of firing; and it seems that the one actually loaded with powder and ball was, by inadvertance, substituted for the weapon prepared for the trick. The bullet crashed through the head of the unfortunate conjurer, who, to the surprise and horror of all present, fell dead upon the stage.

A similar and yet more sad catastrophe darkened the latter years of the conjurer DeLinsky, who enjoyed a considerable repute on the continent at the beginning of the present century. On the 10th of November, 1820, he gave a performance at Arnstadt, in the presence of the family of Prince Schwartzburg-Sondershauser, and wished to bring it off with as much eclat as possible. Six soldiers were introduced, who were to fire with ball cartridges at the young wife of the conjurer, having previously rehearsed their part, and been instructed to bite off the bullet when biting the cartridge, and retain it in the mouth.

This was trusting too much to untrained subordinates, and the result justified the apprehensions of Madame De-Linsky, who is said to have been unwilling to perform the part assigned to her in the trick, and to have assented reluctantly by the persuasion of her husband.

The soldiers drawn up in line in the presence of the spectators, presented their muskets at Madame DeLinsky and fired.

For a moment she remainded standing, but almost immediately sank down, exclaiming, "Dear husband, I am shot."

One of the soldiers had not bitten off the bullet, and it had passed through the abdomen of the unfortunate woman, who never spoke after she fell, and died on the second day after the accident. Many of the spectators fainted when they saw her fall, and the catastrophe gave a shock to DeLinsky which, for a time, impaired his reason. He had recently lost a child, and his unfortunate wife was expecting soon to become a mother again when this terrible event deprived her of life.

A French conjurer of this period, was Comte, who was as famous for his ventriloquial powers as for his skill in legerdemain. Many anecdotes are current among continental conjurers of the consternation which Comte created on various occasions by the exercise of his powers as a ventriloquist off the boards. He once overtook a man near Nerves, who was beating an overladen ass, and throwing his voice in the direction of the poor brute's head, reproached the fellow for his cruelty, causing him to stare at the ass for a moment in mingled surprise and awe, and then take to his heels. On another occasion, being in the market-place of Macon, he inquired the price of a pig which a peasant woman had for sale, and pronounced it extortionate, a charge which the owner, with much volubility, denied.

"I will ask the pig," said Comte, gravely.

"Piggy, is the good woman asking a fair price for you?"

"Too much by half," the pig seemed to reply. "I am measled and she knows it."

The woman gasped and stared, but she was equal to the occasion.

"Oh; the villian," she exclaimed. "He has bewitched my pig; Police, seize the sorcerer."

The bystanders rushed to the spot, but Comte slipped away as quickly as he could, and left the affair to the intelligence of the police.

On one occasion the possession of this strange power was the means of saving Comte's life. He was denounced by some ignorant Swiss peasants in the neighborhood of Friburg as a sorcerer, set upon and beaten with sticks, and was about to be thrown into a lime kiln when he raised such a horrible yell, which appeared to proceed from the kiln, that the fellows dropped him, and fled precipitately from the spot.

On the occasion of his performing before Louis XVIII., he asked the King to draw a card from the pack, at the same time "forcing" the king of hearts, which Louis drew. The card being replaced, and the pack shuffled, Comte presented the King with a card as the one drawn.

"I fancy you have done more than you intended," said Louis with a smile. "I drew the king of hearts, and you have given me a portrait of myself."

"I am right, sire," returned Comte. "Your Majesty is king of hearts of all your faithful subjects."

He then placed the card in the midst of some flowers in a vase, and in a few moments the bust of Louis rose from the bouquet.

John Henry Anderson, who now claims our attention, and who attained a world-wide renown, as the Wizard of the North, was born in Aberdeenshire, and was the son of an operative mason. Losing both his parents while a child, he became his own pilot on the voyage of life at the early age of ten years, in the capacity of call-boy to the theatrical company then performing on the northern circuit, under the management of Mr. Ryder. Natural aptitude for the performance of juggling tricks, and for the construction of curious pieces of mechanism, led him, at the age of seventeen, to adopt the trade of conjurer, his only knowledge of which was derived from an evening's observation of the performance of Ingleby Lunar.

His earliest performances were given in the small towns of the north of Scotland, and his first "hit" was made while performing in the Farmer's Hall, at Brechin, in the spring of 1837. Lord Panmure, who was entertaining a party of friends at Brechin Castle at the time, invited the young conjurer not only to exhibit his skill to the guests, but to dine with them, an invitation which was a source of much trouble of mind to Anderson, though the result was very much to his advantage. Unacquainted as he was with the code of etiquette adopted by the upper ten thousand, he could scarcely fail to commit many offences against it, and many a laugh has been excited by his recital of the solecism of which he was guilty during and after dinner. The kindness of his host and hostess, and the polite good humor of their other guests, spared him any serious unpleasantness, however, and his exertions in entertaining the company with all the best tricks of his then limited repertoire were rewarded with a fee of ten pounds and the following flattering testimonial:

"Sir: Our party here last night witnessed your performance with the greatest satisfaction; and I have no hesitation in saying that you far excel any other necromancer that I ever saw, either at home or abroad.

PANMURE."

Anderson was now richer than he had ever been before, and this unexpected accession of capital gave him, in its prudent use, a new impetus on the path of fame. He had already assumed the imposing title of the Wizard of the North, which he afterwards claimed to have received from Sir Walter Scott, and by which he was afterwards known. The story is, as told by Anderson himself, that the great novelist said to him, after a performance at Abbotsford, "They call me the Wizard of the North, Mr. Anderson, but the title should be borne by you." But, as Scott suffered his first attack of paralysis at the beginning of 1830, and was a physical and mental wreck from that time until his death in 1832, it is not easy to reconcile this story with Anderson's statement, that his performances were confined to the north of Scotland until a period subsequent to his exhibition at Brechin Castle in 1837.

Nearly two years later came Louis Döbler, a young German of prepossessing appearance and gentlemanly manners, who had gained a good repute as a conjurer on the continent, and performed before the Courts of Berlin, Vienna, and St. Petersburg. He engaged the St. James's Theatre for his performances in London, and though unable to speak English, achieved a considerable success. " Herr Dobler," said the critic of the leading journal, "is not one of the common genus of jugglers or conjurers, who by a

series of card, dice, or ball tricks, creates momentary amaze-
ment, which vanishes immediately, but his illusions are o
such a surprising character that they carry the mind of his
audience with him throughout his performance, so inex-
plicable are the mysteries he practices. He is most pleasing
in manner, prepossessing in appearance, and, moreover, i
habited in the style which we are taught to believe apper
tains to those who are supposed to have dealings with
familiar spirits. Anderson, the 'Great Wizard of the
North,' who figured at the Strand, and who was followed
by Jacobs, another celebrated conjurer, was an *artiste,*
possessed of considerable ability in the transformation of
oranges into cocoa-nuts, and could at pleasure and with
little assistance, produce a plum pudding from the hat of
one of his auditory, besides standing up as a target, and
facing the fire of his deadly enemy; but he was unequal to
Herr Dobler. Jacobs can in no manner be compared to
him, for though he could extemporise and ventriloquise to
increase the mirth of an audience, there was wanting in his
magic that finish which gives double effect to that of Herr
Dobler.''

The German conjurer presented an array of glittering
and elaborate apparatus such as had never been seen before;
except on the stage occupied by Anderson. On the table
and cabinets on which the cabalistic implements and vessels
were arranged stood two hundred wax candles, which, or
the rising of the curtain, were unlighted; but on Dobler's
appearance, in the costume of a German student of the
fifteenth century, and discharging a pistol, they burst simul-
taneously into illumination. With this sensational intro
duction, the conjurer proceeded to execute the marvels
promised in his programme.

The first that attracted marked attention was the bottle
trick, performed in a new manner. Filling a common wine
bottle with water, he transformed the water into a collection
of wines of various countries, and poured out a glass of each
in succession. Then when all the wine had been emptied
he broke the bottle, and extracted from it a silk handkerchief, the property of a gentleman in the pit, who had previously seen it deposited on a table at the back of the stage.
A pack of cards was then handed to a gentleman, who

having taken note of one, handed them back to the conjurer, by whom they were flung into the air, and the selected card pierced with a small sword as they fell confusedly toward the stage.

Dobler then obtained a watch from a lady in the stalls, placed it one side and presented the owner with a ball wrapped in a towel. He then placed an orange in a small silver vase, which stood on one of the tables. The ball was afterwards found in the vase, and the orange in the towel held by the lady; and upon the orange being cut open, the watch was found in it. Two handkerchiefs presented by persons in the stalls were enclosed in vases, and immediately underwent an invisible transit from one to the other. Upon the conjurer firing a pistol, they were found to have both disappeared, and, upon looking up in the direction of his aim, they were seen dangling from the ceiling. Another shot brought them down, almost into their owners' laps.

Dobler's ''Gypsies' Wonder Kitchen,'' a very simple trick but which, when well managed, never fails to draw immense applause, puzzled the spectators more than anything else. An iron pot was suspended from a tripod, and several pigeons, prepared for cooking, were placed in it, with sufficient water to boil them. Fire was then applied by means of a spirit lamp placed beneath the pot, and when the culinary operation was supposed to be completed, the lid was raised, and as many living pigeons flew out of the pot as there had been dead ones placed in it.

Another novel trick was the miraculous washing, in which eight or ten handkerchiefs, borrowed for the occasion, were, to all appearance, immersed in water, put through the process of ablution, and thrown into the rinsing tub. The conjurer then fired a pistol, and, on opening a box on another table, which had previously been shown to be empty, discovered the handkerchiefs, dried, ironed, and as neatly folded as if they had just come from the laundress. After this came the cornucopia trick, which Dobler performed with an old hat, from which, after first exhibiting it in a state of utter inanity, and trampling it under his feet, he produced an apparently inexhaustible supply of tiny bouquets of flowers, which he threw to the ladies in stalls, pit, and boxes; and with this floral shower brought his entertainment to a close.

Dobler performed before the Queen and the Royal family at Windsor Castle shortly after his arrival in England, and on the conclusion of his London season made a successfu tour of the principal towns of the midland and northern counties, and extended it to Edinburgh and Glasgow. His last performance at the St. James's Theatre was signalized by the presentation to every occupant of the stalls and boxes of a copy of the following farewell verses, in German and English :

> Forth from my German land I came,
>   The pilgrim's staff alone I bore ;
> Stranger alike in speech and fame,
>   I sought proud Albion's friendly shore.

> Some happy months have passed—I find
>   Farewell as cordial waits me now
> As first I found your welcome kind ;
>   Let warmest thanks my debts avow.

> You judged my humble toil to please
>   With such a gently voice and smile,
> The stranger scarce were more at ease
>   If born upon your honored Isle.

> With sorrow then my eye must view
>   The parting which this night must bring ;
> And even a tear may gem, like dew,
>   The latest " floral gifts " I fling.

> My hand this charmed verse has traced—
>   'Tis what my heart must long contain—
> Prayer—in your memories to be placed,
>   And hope—that we may meet again.

In the summer of 1845, three years after the departure of Dobler, a French conjurer appeared at the St. James's, and afterwards at the Strand, under the name of Philippe. His true name was Philip Talon, under which he had been, prior to his adoption of the conjuring profession, engaged in the confectionery trade. He was born at Alais, near Nismes, and going to Paris, as many provincials do, in the hope of making a fortune, or at the worst, realizing a competency, proved the truth of the adage that " all that glitters is not gold," and betook himself to London. There he was equally unsuccessful, and removed by a singular choice, to Aberdeen.

There was a theatrical company performing in Aberdeen, but drawing so badly that the receipts failed to pay their salaries and they were, from the manager to the call-boy, in the same plight as the poor Frenchman.

Talon proposed that two or three more performances should be given, and that every person entering the theatre should receive with the check, a packet of confectionery and a ticket entitling him or her to participate in a lottery drawing for a sum of fifteen pounds. The announcement of this scheme produced crowded houses, and after the final performance, Talon found that he had cleared off his stock of confectionery, and was the possessor of a sum of money more than sufficient to provide himself with a modest set of conjuring apparatus.

He now assumed the name of Philippe, under which he traveled through Scotland and England, visiting all the principal towns, at first performing only the ordinary tricks of all the itinerant conjurers, but gradually extending his repertoire, and improving his manipulation by study and practice.

The chief attractions at Philippe's entertainment in London were the gold-fish trick and a trio of ingeniously contrived automatons. This gold-fish trick was at that time a novelty, not having been performed by Jacobs until five years later.

Philippe threw a shawl in the air, to show that it enclosed nothing, and, catching it as it descended, wrapped it around him. In an instant he withdrew it, and discovered at his feet a glass globe, brimful of water, in which four gold fish were swimming. In a few moments the process was repeated, and another bowl, similarly filled, was produced. He then stepped forward to a platform between the orchestra and the stalls, and there discovered a third globe of fish; and returning to the stage, without the least apparant communication with anything or anybody, brought to light, in the same mysterious manner, half-a-dozen live ducks, and finally, a couple of geese which walked gravely about the stage.

Wiljalba Frikell, who also made his first appearance in London in 1851, is the next claimant of our attention. He was born in 1818, at Scopio, a village in Finland, on the borders of Lapland. His parents being in good circumstances, he was well educated, completing his studies at the high school of Munich, which he did not leave until 1840, when in his twenty-second year. He practised legerdemain while studying, as his parents hoped, for one of the learned professions, and read all the works on the subject that he could obtain, but on the completion of his collegiate career, the love of travel combined with his conjuring proclivities, induced him to set out on a tour through eastern and southern Europe as a professor of the Black Art.

He traveled through Germany, Hungary, Wallachia and Turkey, and thence proceeded to Egypt, where he had the honor of performing before Mehemet Ali, who awarded him a gold medal for his proficiency in the magical art. Returning to Europe he visited Greece, Italy and Spain, and afterwards proceeded to India. In all of the countries he visited, he took care to see the performances of all the conjurers whom he had found engaged in the exercise of their profession, and devoted much time to the study and practice of the means of dispensing with apparatus.

"The use of complicated and cumbrous apparatus," he observed in the preface of his "LESSONS IN MAGIC," "to which modern conjurers have become addicted, not only greatly diminishes the amount of astonishment they are enabled to produce—a defect which is not compensated by the external splendor and imposing effect of such paraphernalia—but the useful lesson, how fallible our senses are, by means the most ordinary and at everybody's command, is entirely lost. It has been my object in my performances to restore the art to its original prominence, and to extend that to a degree which it has, I believe, never yet hitherto reached. I banish all such mechanical and scientific preparatives from my own practice, confining myself for the most part to the objects and materials of every-day life. The success which I have met with emboldens me to believe that I have followed the right path."

On his return to Europe from the East, he traveled through Russia, Sweden and Denmark, and performed before the royal families of those countries. The Czar presented him with a valuable diamond ring, and the King of Denmark decorated him with the order of the Dannebrog.

In 1851 he came to London as already stated, and performed at the Hanover Square Rooms, and afterwards at the St. James's Theatre. The absence of apparatus was a novelty, though it is probable the greater part of his auditors would have been impressed in a greater degree, by such a lavish display of glittering apparatus as had been made by Anderson and Jacobs. His broken German and a comical peculiarity of manner caused him to be described in PUNCH as " a comic Charles Matthews;" and as he did not follow the examples of Dobler and Phillipe in the matter of costume, the critic of the same facetious publication compared him to " a monster raven in full dress for an evening party."

The next professor of note was Bosco, a native of Lombardy, where he was born in 1823. Like Frikell, he received a liberal education, and studied medicine, in which he obtained a diploma; but his professional prospects being injured by his participation in the revolutionary movement against the Austrian domination in 1848, he was led by the success of his performances as an amateur conjurer to make legerdemain his profession. Travelling through Piedmont and Switzerland, and afterwards visiting the principal towns of Germany, he at length reached Berlin, where he had the honor of performing before the King of Prussia and the Royal family.

From Berlin he ventured to proceed to Vienna, where also, his antecedents being forgotten or unknown, he performed before the Imperial Court. Another tour of Germany brought him in 1854 to the Rhine again; he travelled westward until Paris was reached, and he was invited to exhibit his skill before the Emperor, who presented him with the cross of the Legion of Honor.

Bosco had as remarkable an aptitude for languages as for legerdemain, and was a most accomplished linguist, having acquired French, Spanish, German, Polish, Russian, Hungarian, Servian, Wallachian and Turkish, in addition to Italian and Latin. Most conjurers are content to address a foreign audience in their own language and we once heard an Indian professor of the art discourse fluently in Hindustanee while performing a trick before an English audience. Dobler could speak only German, and the broken English

of Frikell was little more intelligible.   Robert Houdin could
speak only French, and when an auditor in the pit, while he
was performing at Manchester, desired him to speak English,
his attempts to render himself intelligible in that language
proved almost as amusing as his tricks.

Bosco was the last of the great conjurers by whom the
public had been amused for twenty years.   The superior
style of the entertainments which they presented, and the
succession of startling feats which compelled the wonder
and admiration of those who witnessed them, made them a
popular means of amusement during that period; but sight-
seers began at length to regard the bills of a new conjurer
with comparative indifference and to ask, with Solomon,
"is there anything whereof it may be said, see, this is new?"

Mr. Alfred Stodare, the new aspirant for public favor,
was a well educated Frenchman, and produced a programme
well spiced with sensational, and therefore highly attractive
feats.   Among them was the Indian basket trick, performed
with a young lady, who entered a large basket, into which
the conjurer thrusts a sword, and from which, on its being
opened, she was found to have vanished, to reappear among
the spectators.   He also performed the trick of the instan-
taneous growth of flowers.

Stodare's greatest marvel, however, was the mysterious
Sphinx.   Upon what appeared to be an ordinary three-
legged table standing in the centre of the stage, a head
stood, reminding the spectator of the famous brazen head
ascribed to Roger Bacon.   The spectator seeing only a head,
and feeling satisfied that there was an open space between
the table and the stage, was amazed when the eyes and lips
moved, and the tongue spoke.

Professor Louis Haselmayer, "Prince of Prestidigitators,
Magician, Necromancer, Musician, and Educator of Birds,"
was born in Vienna, Austria, on the 18th September, 1839.
For a period of ten years, nothing of moment occurred in
his career that is worth mentioning, save and except that
from his earliest childhood his character developed a passion
for mechanical pursuits, which foreshadowed his future
career.   From ten to fifteen years of age, his whole time
was occupied in completing his education at the College at
Vienna, from which place he graduated at the early age of

eighteen. All his leisure time during the latter years of his collegiate curriculum, was devoted to the study and working of mechanical illusions and magical apparatus, and from the years 1857 to 1861, his services were constantly in demand among the aristocratic families of the Austrian capital, in giving his " *Soirees de Magique.*" During this period his performances were witnessed several times in person by Francis Joseph, Emperor of Austria, and at the close of one of his entertainments, he was presented with a medal of art of knowledge by his Imperial Majesty in person, for his—even at that time—numerous and clever inventions, amongst which was an entirely novel musical apparatus, composed exclusively of wood and india rubber, and called by him the "Stylocarfe." During the latter months of 1864, while giving a private performance, Professor Haselmayer chanced to have among his audience a well-known prestidigitator, who was so impressed with the marvellous illusions he then saw, that he immediately made propositions to join in a professional tour through the United States. This Professor Haselmayer at last consented to, and they opened at the Academy of Music, New York, in September, 1865. After exhibiting in New York, Professor Haselmayer made a tour of the country, and then went to Australia and the East Indies, and when last heard of was in South Africa. The following acrostic on his name is from the pen of one of his admirers.

ACROSTIC.

Hey ; presto ; pass ; the modern Prosp'ro cries :
At his command his faithful Ariel flies ;
Swift through the air he wings his noiseless way ;
Excels himself his master to obey.
Lo ; now the sprite assumes some novel shape ;
Mark how the crowding mortals gaze agape ;
Amazed, astounded, struck with wonder dumb,
Yet fearing naught, whatever change may come ;
Enchanter, may thy spells that charm us so,
Reap rich reward wherever thou shalt go.

We now see Dr. Lynn, whose long successful season in London was quite remarkable. Although his apparatus is less elaborate than that of Anderson and Robert Houdin, he does not agree with Frikell in disregarding it altogether, and still less in the Finnish conjurers' disregard of the art of language. "He is," to quote the words of one of his London critics, "a most accomplished master of the whole art of humbug, and he does his humbugging with such ease and neatness, such self possession and invulnerable effrontery, that one must envy the man if he experiences one-half the pleasure in cheating his audience that his audience does in being cheated. From the moment he comes to the front with his wand, this plump magician keeps the attention of all in the room enchained; his restless eyes sparkle from side to side, his nimble tongue patters with the rapidity of a Wheatstone transmitter, and his magic fingers are diving into the secrets of unconscious pockets. There have been other wizards with powers as great, possibly greater, in their peculiar lines, but the specialty of Lynn, in which he excels all of them, is his marvelous talkee-talkee. He cracks a joke, tells an anecdote, or bandies a repartee, always effective, and all this time he is working his wonders, for his running fire of remark is less to tickle the listeners than to divert their notice from the trick he is performing. He deludes the most watchful spectator, as he lucidly explains, 'that is how it is done.'"

The wonderful career of Maskelyne and Cooke of Egyptian Hall, London, is so well known to our readers through other writers, that we only take up space to give here their latest programme, the main features of which are now being produced in this country by Prof. Harry Kellar.

EGYPTIAN HALL,

—LONDON.—

-::-ENGLAND'S HOME OF MYSTERY-::-

Messrs.

MASKELYNE

and

COOKE'S

——ENTERTAINMENT.——

(Sole Proprietor, Mr. J. N. Maskelyne.

Twenty-second Consecutive Year in London.

PROGRAMME.

Price One Penny.

PROGRAMME.

Fifteen Minutes of Elegant Jugglery by Mr. Maskelyne.

—::— —::— —::— —::— —::—

Selection; Metzler's Organo Piano.)

Mr. F. Cramer.

Members of the audience desirous of inspecting the mechanism of this beautiful instrument, may do so by applying to Mr. Cramer at the conclusion of the performance.

—::— —::— —::— —::— —::—

THE ARTIST'S DREAM.

A Romance Mystique.

Invented by Mr. Devant, written by Mr. Spurr, the mechanism devised and constructed by Mr. Maskelyne.

Maurice, (an Artist)   -   -   -   Mr. J. B. Hansard
Ellaline (his Spirit Wife)   -   -   Miss Marion Melvelle
Spirit of Mercy   -   -   -   -   Miss Olive Elton

—::— —::— —::— —::— —::—

An Object Lesson in Sleight of Hand.

by

MR. DAVID DEVANT.

One of the most accomplished exponents of this fascinating art of the present day.

Mr. Devant possesses the commendable quality so rarely to be found in modern Conjurers, viz., absolute originality; every experiment he performs has been invented by himself.

A Series of Wonderful & Laughable Electric Hand Shadows.

—::— —::— —::— —::— —::—

A New and Original Magical Sketch, entitled

MODERN WITCHERY.

Invented by Mr. J. N. Maskelyne, written by Mr. Nevil Maskelyne. Founded upon facts connected with the political movement called Theosophy.

Professor Zoorooster (an adept)   -   Mr. Nevil Maskelyne
Countess Blarni (President of the Beervatskin Lodge of
   Theosophists)   -   -   -   Mr. J. B. Hansard
Martha Toogood (a Woman with a mission)
   -   -   -   -   -   -   Miss Olive Elton
William Toogood (a Henpecked Husband)
   -   -   -   -   -   -   Mr. W. F. Brooke
Christofolo (alias Koot Hoomi, a Mahatma)   Mr. E. Elton

NOTE.—The views expressed by the characters in this Sketch are by
no means exaggerations of their Theosophical originals; the
doctrine is sufficiently absurd for an amusing sketch. The
pretended miracles upon which Theosophy was founded,
however, are too childish to be reproduced upon the stage of
the Egyptian Hall, consequently Mr. Maskelyne has had to
rely entirely upon his own invention to supply the illusory
portions of the sketch. "The Miracle of Lh'asa" and "The
Astral appearance of Koot Hoomi" will rank among the
most inscrutable mysteries ever produced.

Professor Antonio Blitz relates the following in his
memoirs which are now out of print.

"My first appearance before an English public took place
at Dover, in December, 1825. The room was very well
filled by quite a respectable audience, who, whatever might
have been their expectations as to what they were to see for
their two shillings during the performance, at its close
became so wonderstruck, that many had very serious
thoughts as to whose company they had been in; and there
were not a small portion of this, my first English audience,
who felt quite serious misgivings as to my being of mortal
make.

Of course their astonishment soon found utterance, and
not many days passed before the "young stranger" enjoyed a very wide reputation; and tales were told of my
doings, and affirmed to be by the church wardens and beadles,
which left but little need, on my part, of other assistance to
notify the public, and my new friends in particular, of what
they would see in honoring my performance by their attend-
ance.

As I passed along the streets, I would be followed by
crowds, all very anxious to get a look at me, and enjoy some
of my peculiar favors, for I was, among the lower classes,

believed to be capable of doing anything, and to enjoy my favors was not an item to be treated lightly.

I soon found myself in business, for besides my stated performances, there were many who sought me out to gain favors for their own personal benefit, and I was requested to do all sorts of things. One poor fellow offered me a few shillings to restore his sick child to health; another wished for a coat; another, a young lady, wished to know as to the truthfulness of an absent lover; while still others, on whom Sir Cupid as yet seemed to have no special favors to bestow, anxious to solve all doubts, sought the all-talked-of magician to know whether love had anything in store for them.

Every event or circumstance which had occurred, was brought for solution, and there were not a few who possessed credulity enough to believe that I had the power to grant each and every favor, and to set all mysterious doings and doubtful matters right. From the smaller provincial towns, we made our way into the cities, and, after being in England some four or five months, I arrived at, and made my first bow in the city of Exeter, (where my reputation had preceded me), in the early part of 1826. When the good bishop heard that I had really come under his very nose, he was not at all pleased with the idea, and bethought himself how I was to be avoided. He knew of no better way than to preach and prejudice the people against me. So, on my arrival, there was a general notice given for all good Christian men and women to avoid seeing, or in any way having anything to do with a mischievous lad, who, by his performances, was leading the heads and hearts of all the people astray.

Such an announcement, whatever might have been the idea of the reverend archbishop, did but little to allay the excitement, and the curiosity of all became from such a proceeding doubly aroused. I, on the other hand, felt, as the bishop seemed to regard me as a person of so much importance, that it was my duty if possible, to maintain my position. Accordingly, I in return gave information that I would cause a watch to be transported from my exhibition room to the "Lady's Pulpit" in the cathedral on such an evening.

The evening came, and, nothwithstanding the notice of

the bishop, as many came to witness this astonishing feat as the place could hold.

At my request persons were appointed on the part of the audience to watch me narrowly, while others were to visit the cathedral at the appointed signal and procure the watch. Of course all my operations were most closely examined.

The feat was to be performed by a pistol being loaded by any one of the persons appointed; the watch to be hung in a position where it could be seen by all; and when I fired at it, it should disappear, and then the others were to start immediately for the cathedral, where the watch should be found, as I promised, under a cushion lying upon the "Lady's Pulpit."

In fulfillment of this assertion, after the pistol was discharged, the committee started for the cathedral, and found the watch just as I had said it should be, in the very place named, under the cushion lying upon the pulpit of "Our Lady." It would be impossible to describe the excitement which this feat occasioned. All Exeter was in an uproar, and the bishop, together with all connected with him, became as much at a loss as to who this very singular being was, as the rest; but they were determined that his performances should not go on. They contended that it would not do for Christians to see such things, and every interest of the church demanded that they should be put an end to at once, by an appeal to the ecclesiastical court. Before this body I was summoned to appear and give an answer as to who I was and by what agency or instrumentalities I was enabled to do such strange and mysterious performances." (Space will not allow us to give in detail the clever manner in which Prof. Blitz acquitted himself at this trial, suffice to say, he came out of it with "flying colors.")

On my arrival in New York, I found that hall accomodations were inconvenient, for the only one of any magnitude I could obtain was Masonic Hall, on Broadway, opposite the hospital. At this place I made my *debut* before an American audience. The public places of amusement then open to the citizens, were the Park and Bowery Theatres, and Niblo's Garden.

Notwithstanding the novelty of my entertainments had

been anticipated in a measure by Monsieur Adrien, a very talented and ingenious Frenchman, I experienced the most unbounded success and flattering countenance from the inhabitants at large; but, while I was patronized for my ability to please and astonish, there was, with a very slight exception, a total absence of an approach to the superstitious character which had constantly marked my progress through the " Old Country."

For weeks and months I continued the recipient of crowded houses. The practical magician was but little understood. The great improvements in mechanical inventions, the elaborate perfection and effect with which feats were presented to the audiences, produced much sensation, and established the superiority of the modern performers, so that in a brief time professors of magic arose in abundance. Adriens and Blitzes were represented in all parts of the country. This circumstance is to be explained from the supposition that the business was profitable and capable of being successfully pursued. Frequently my identity has been disputed when I have visited the different towns and cities professionally. In later years this has proved an incalculable annoyance, there being not less than thirteen people travelling the country using my name and profession, circulating 'a verbatim copy of my handbill and advertisement—not only assuming to be the original Blitz, but in many instances claiming to be a son or nephew. I have been in constant receipt of bills of their contracting, for not content with taking my name, they have not even not enough to pay their debts. The thirteen now travelling in the United States exhibit under the following and other names:—

Signor Blitz.
Signor Blitz, Jr.
Signor Blitz, The Original.
Signor Blitz's Son.
Signor Blitz's Nephew.
Signor Blitz, The Great.
Signor Blitz, The Wonderful.
Signor Blitz, The Unrivalled.
Signor Blitz, The Mysterious.
Signor Blitz, By Purchase.
Signor Blitz, The Great Original.

The greatest annoyance attending the movements of these impostors was, and is yet; the constant flood of writs, judgments and bills served upon me for payment, or to enforce payment of claims these men had contracted and neglected to settle. Such demands have proved sorely grievous, from the fact that I have ever adopted the rule of promptly discharging all my professional indebtedness.

Speaking of the gun trick, this feat was the most adroit in my performance; and, while it created a marked sensation and interest to the rough and unpolished, it was never popular with the refined and feeling; and, finally, it became attended with so much danger, that I found it necessary for self protection to abandon it."

During the '60's many conjurers were introducing in their performances the "Bullet Proof Artist," and many of them created quite a sensation. One particularly, Prof. Epstein in Germany, drew full houses with this attraction.

The fear and anxiety for the magician's life, as well as curiosity to see how the shot was fired at him, without doing any injury, attracted the public to these performances.

. The magician realizing that to keep curiosity alive would be the means of pecuniary success to him, proceeded to utilize his knowledge to the best advantage, and in this he succeeded. But the secret of the trick had finally become known and this caused it to lose its attraction.

While at a watering place Prof. Epstein took sick and it was soon rumored that he had been accidentally shot during one of his performances, and that his case was almost hopeless.

A great deal of sympathy was entertained for him, especially by those who had witnessed his performances. Everybody talked about the accident and expressed their sorrow for the unfortunate professor. He was mentioned as being a very skillful performer, &c.; in a few days the papers published the fact that Prof. Epstein had been accidentally shot during one of his interesting exhibitions.

It is unnecessary to state that this was only an advertising scheme to attract public attention. At first it worked like a charm; people were unaccustomed to exaggerations of the press. When it was reported that his recovery was expected in the near future, friends, to show their sympathy, commenced making preparations for his reappearance. The Casino was not large enough to accommodate the spectators, and instead of one performance, three had to be given.

He thought it advisable not to exhibit the shooting trick on this occasion, and the hero (?) of the evening entertained and amused his appreciative audience with other experiments of his skill.

When the magician made his appearance at other places, things were quite different, the public grew suspicious, felt itself deceived and did not quite believe in the resurrection of a magician who had been shot. From that time Prof. Epstein was "dead to the world."

Here and there other magicians assumed his name, to profit from his fame, but they too had to discover that they were sadly mistaken. This seems to be a peculiarity of magicians. There have been several who travelled under the name of Prof. Hermann, and, of course, all claimed to be that most famous of magicians, "the renowned Prof. Hermann of Vienna."

People would take advantage of the opportunity to admire this great artist of whose skill and dexterity so much had been heard, and who happened to stop at their place during his travels. Very often the pretended Hermann, assisted by the press, and the real Hermann's reputation, would profit by this.

But very few among the audience discovered that the performer was an imposter, as Prof. Hermann rarely appeared in the places frequented by these "would-be-Hermann's."

Audiences in small places did not as a rule know Hermann personally, who condescended to give a performance "by special request."

Great things were anticipated, and the disappointment of the spectators can be imagined, when the performer exhibited tricks which had been seen at the ordinary fairs for years.

Such actions on the part of unscrupulous magicians are the main cause of the decadence of this very interesting but harmless art.

Every magician ought to, by practice, endeavor to be.

come perfect, and when having won fame to retain it, then he or she will always be received as a welcome guest. If you cannot carve out your own reputation, based on your originality and skill, you cannot make it by imitating or trading on the reputation of another.—

As the life and works of Robert Houdin, that "Leader of Conjurers," are no doubt well known to our readers, we have not mentioned him in this article; and as the writings of Professor Hoffmann and others, have done so much to bring out the history and feats of modern French and American conjurers we feel that further consideratien of these interesting subjects must be left for some future work.*

------

*The careers of Robert Heller, Alexander Hermann, Harry Kellar, and other conjurers familiar to Americans are found in the book, "Leaves from Conjurers' Scrap Books" or "Modern Magicians and their Works," by the same author.—

www.ingramcontent.com/pod-product-compliance
Lightning Source LLC
Chambersburg PA
CBHW021545270326
41930CB00008B/1365